LAUGH-OUT-LOUD
JOKES

LAUGH-OUT-LOUD ANIMAL JOKES

CAITIE MCANENEY

WINDMILL BOOKS

Published in 2025 by Windmill Books, an Imprint of Rosen Publishing
2544 Clinton St., Buffalo, NY 14224

First Edition

Editor: Caitie McAneney
Book Design: Claire Zimmermann

Photo Credits: Cover, p.1 (child laughing) mimagephotography/Shutterstock.com; series art (animal illustrations) Nadzin/Shutterstock.com, (paper texture) OanaGherghe2/Shutterstock.com; p. 5 Martin Valigursky/Shutterstock.com; p. 7 Georgia Evans/Shutterstock.com; p. 9 (cat) Kasefoto/Shutterstock.com; p. 9 (tiger) Ondrej Prosicky/Shutterstock.com; p. 11 Avigator Fortuner/Shutterstock.com; p. 13 UNIKYLUCKK/Shutterstock.com; p. 15 BublikHaus/Shutterstock.com; p. 17 Andreas Lippenberger/Shutterstock.com; p. 19 Oakland Images/Shutterstock.com; p. 21 DWI YULIANTO/Shutterstock.com.

Library of Congress Cataloging-in-Publication Data

Names: McAneney, Caitie, author.
Title: Laugh-out-loud animal jokes / Caitie McAneney.
Description: Buffalo : Windmill Books, 2025. | Series: Laugh-out-loud jokes | Includes index.
Identifiers: LCCN 2024004368 (print) | LCCN 2024004369 (ebook) | ISBN 9781538396834 (library binding) | ISBN 9781538396827 (paperback) | ISBN 9781538396841 (ebook)
Subjects: LCSH: Animals–Juvenile humor. | Wit and humor, Juvenile.
Classification: LCC PN6231.A5 M33 2024 (print) | LCC PN6231.A5 (ebook) | DDC 808.88/2-dc23/eng/20240130
LC record available at https://lccn.loc.gov/2024004368
LC ebook record available at https://lccn.loc.gov/2024004369

Manufactured in the United States of America

CPSIA Compliance Information: Batch #CSWM25. For further information, contact Rosen Publishing at 1-800-237-9932

CONTENTS

Words in the glossary appear in **bold** the first time they are used in the text.

ANIMALS GONE WILD!

What animals like to take baths?

SHAMPOODLES!

Why shouldn't you play cards on the savanna?

THERE ARE TOO MANY CHEETAHS!

Did you hear about the funny owl?

HE WAS A HOOT!

What do you do if your pet chews your book?

TAKE THE WORDS OUT OF ITS MOUTH!

FUN FACT!

The first animals to be **domesticated** were dogs. They were tamed by people in Central Asia about 15,000 years ago.

BEAR-Y GOOD JOKES!

What do you call a bear with no teeth?

A GUMMY BEAR!

What's a bear's favorite dessert?

BLUEBEARY PIE!

What do you call bears with no ears?

B!

What do you call a bear that's caught in the rain?

A DRIZZLY BEAR!

FUN FACT!

A grizzly bear can run at speeds of up to 35 miles (56 km) per hour. That's as fast as the speed limit for cars in many towns!

MEOW-MAZING HUMOR

Why do cats always win video games?

THEY HAVE NINE LIVES!

What's a cat's favorite color?

PURR-PLE!

Where do cats go for fun?

A MEWSEUM.

Why did the cat want a guitar?

TO PLAY SOME MEWSIC.

FUN FACT!

House cats share more than 95 percent of their **DNA** with tigers! About 10.8 million years ago, house cats and tigers split and became different animals.

ELEPHANT ENTERTAINMENT

What weighs two tons and wears glass slippers?

CINDERELLEPHANT!

Why is an elephant's skin so wrinkly?

YOU CAN'T IRON THEM!

How do elephants call one another?

ON THE ELE-PHONE!

Why aren't elephants allowed in swimming pools?

THEIR TRUNKS ALWAYS FALL DOWN.

FUN FACT!

Elephants spend up to 18 hours a day eating! They also make about a ton of poop each week.

BUNNY BITS

What is a bunny's favorite song?

"DON'T WORRY, BE HOPPY"

What do you get if you cross a rabbit and an ant?

BUGS BUNNY.

How can you find a group of old rabbits?

LOOK FOR GRAY HARES!

Can rabbits dance?

ONLY IF IT'S HIP-HOP!

FUN FACT!

Rabbits are great at jumping. They can jump nearly 3 feet (1 m) high in one leap!

PLAYFUL PUPS

Why was the dog sad?

IT WAS HAVING A RUFF DAY.

Can dogs tell time?

A WATCH DOG CAN!

What do you call a dog who loves the snow?

A SLUSH PUPPY!

What kind of dog sneezes a lot?

ACHOO-WAWA!

FUN FACT!

A dog's sense of smell is 40 times stronger than a human's! Some dogs are used to find things for police **investigations.**

BIRD NERDS

What do you give a bird queen?

THE ROYAL TWEETMENT.

Why do hummingbirds hum?

THEY DON'T KNOW THE WORDS TO THE SONG.

Are pet birds expensive?

NO, THEY'RE CHEEP!

Why did the rooster cross the road?

TO SHOW EVERYONE HE WASN'T A CHICKEN!

FUN FACT!

More than 10,000 **species** of birds live on Earth! All birds have feathers and lay eggs. However some birds, like ostriches, cannot fly.

MONKEYING AROUND

What did the monkey bring to the party?

CHIMPS AND DIP.

What do you get when you mix a **primate** with a **crustacean**?

A SHRIMP-ANZEE!

What was the angry monkey's name?

FURIOUS GEORGE.

How do you open a banana?

JUST USE A MON-KEY!

FUN FACT!

Monkeys are very smart! They often live together in groups, **communicate** with one another, and solve problems.

LIZARD LAUGHS

What do you call a lizard who likes hip-hop?

A RAP-TILE.

What kinds of shoes do reptiles like best?

CROCS!

What did the chameleon say to her son on his first day at a new school?

"DON'T WORRY! YOU'LL BLEND RIGHT IN."

What do you call a crime-fighting reptile?

AN INVESTI-GATOR.

FUN FACT!

Lizards have some amazing **defenses**! Some can change color to match their surroundings, like chameleons. Others can lose their tail to get away from predators!

GLOSSARY

communicate: To share ideas and feelings through sounds and motions.

crustacean: An animal with a hard shell, jointed limbs, feelers, and no backbone.

defense: A feature of a living thing that helps keep it safe.

domesticated: Bred and raised for use by people.

DNA: Part of the body that carries genetic information, which gives the instructions for life.

furious: Very angry.

investigation: An ordered search for facts about something.

primate: Any animal from the group that includes humans, apes, and monkeys.

savanna: A grassland with scattered patches of trees.

species: A group of plants or animals that are all the same kind.

FOR MORE INFORMATION

BOOKS

Clasky, Leonard. *Let's Tell Jokes About Dogs.* Buffalo, NY: Windmill Books, 2023.

Elliott, Rob. *The Big Book of Knock-Knock Jokes.* New York, NY: Harper Collins Publishers, 2022.

King, Joe. *Punny Jokes.* Minneapolis, MN: Abdo Kids Junior, 2022.

WEBSITES

Animal Jokes
www.ducksters.com/jokes/animals.php
Check out more animal jokes to make your friends laugh!

Knock-Knock Animal Jokes
www.highlightskids.com/jokes/jokes/Knock-Knock-animal-jokes
Explore silly knock-knock jokes from Highlights Kids.

Publisher's note to educators and parents: Our editors have carefully reviewed these websites to ensure that they are suitable for students. Many websites change frequently, however, and we cannot guarantee that a site's future contents will continue to meet our high standards of quality and educational value. Be advised that students should be closely supervised whenever they access the internet.

INDEX